Buddy BOOKS
Prehistoric Animals

Woolly Mammoth

ABDO
Publishing Company

A Buddy Book
by
Michael P. Goecke

D1205487

VISIT US AT
www.abdopub.com

Published by Buddy Books, an imprint of ABDO Publishing Company, 4940 Viking Drive, Edina, Minnesota 55435. Copyright © 2003 by Abdo Consulting Group, Inc. International copyrights reserved in all countries. No part of this book may be reproduced in any form without written permission from the publisher.

Printed in the United States.

Edited by: Christy DeVillier
Contributing Editor: Matt Ray
Graphic Design: Deborah Coldiron
Image Research: Deborah Coldiron
Illustrations: Deborah Coldiron, Denise Esner
Photographs: Corbis, Corel, Steve McHugh, Photodisc

Library of Congress Cataloging-in-Publication Data

Goecke, Michael P., 1968-
    Woolly Mammoth / Michael P. Goecke.
        p. cm. — (Prehistoric animal Set I)
    Includes index.
    Summary: Introduces the physical characteristics, habitat, and behavior of the prehistoric relative of modern-day Indian elephants.
    ISBN 1-57765-971-6
    1. Woolly mammoth—Juvenile literature. [1. Woolly mammoth. 2. Mammoths.] I. Title.

QE882.P8 G64 2003
569'.6—dc21

2002028193

Table of Contents

Prehistoric Animals

Anything that was around before 5,500 years ago is prehistoric. Scientists study fossils to learn about prehistoric life. Fossils help them understand the prehistoric world.

Dinosaurs were prehistoric animals. They died out about 65 million years ago. Mammals became common after the dinosaurs. Some prehistoric mammals were saber-toothed cats, giant sloths, and mammoths.

Prehistoric Animals

The Woolly Mammoth

Mammoths were prehistoric elephants. They are famous for their long tusks. There were ancestral, steppe, Columbian, and woolly mammoths. The smallest of these was the woolly mammoth.

Scientists have names for important time periods in Earth's history. The woolly mammoth lived during a time period called the Pleistocene. The Pleistocene began about two million years ago.

A Geologic Timeline
248 Million Years Ago – Today

Triassic	Jurassic	Cretaceous	Paleocene	Eocene	Oligocene	Miocene	Pliocene	Pleistocene	Holocene
248 – 213 Million Years Ago	213 – 145 Million Years Ago	145 – 65 Million Years Ago	65 – 56 Million Years Ago	56 – 34 Million Years Ago	34 – 24 Million Years Ago	24 – 5 Million Years Ago	5 – 2 Million Years Ago	2 Million – 11,500 Years Ago	11,500 Years Ago – Today

Age Of Dinosaurs	Age Of Mammals
248 – 65 Million Years Ago	65 Million Years Ago – Today

Woolly mammoths lived between 500,000 and 10,000 years ago.

What It Looked Like

Woolly mammoths were as big as today's African elephants. They grew to become about 10 feet (3 m) tall. Adult males probably weighed as much as eight tons (seven t).

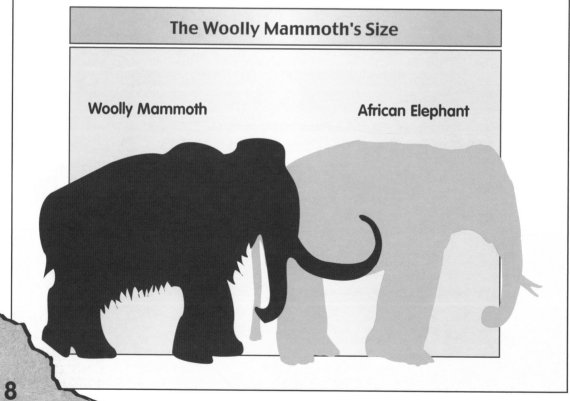

The Woolly Mammoth's Size

Woolly Mammoth

African Elephant

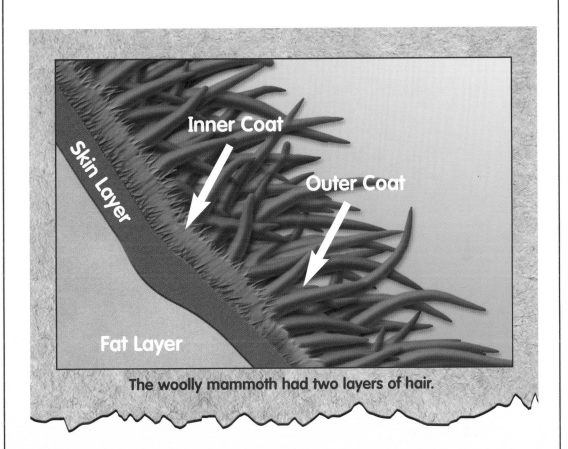

Inner Coat

Outer Coat

Skin Layer

Fat Layer

The woolly mammoth had two layers of hair.

Unlike today's elephants, the woolly mammoth was very hairy. It had two coats of hair. An inner coat of short hair grew near its skin. Its outer coat was long and shaggy. Some hairs were three feet (one m) long.

People have found many woolly mammoth tusk fossils.

Both male and female woolly mammoths had tusks. Tusks are long teeth. A woolly mammoth's curved tusks could grow to become 13 feet (4 m) long.

The woolly mammoth was a prehistoric elephant.

11

Like elephants today, the woolly mammoth had a trunk. Its ears were small. The woolly mammoth also had a hump on its back. This hump stored fat.

Woolly Mammoth

Today's camels have humps that store fat, too.

Columbian Mammoth

Woolly Mammoth

Columbian Mammoth

The Columbian mammoth was a bit different from the woolly mammoth. It was bigger and did not have a hairy coat. The Columbian mammoth only lived in North America.

All elephants eat plants. The woolly mammoth ate grasses and leaves. It may have eaten leaves from willow, fir, and alder trees. The woolly mammoth probably ate about 400 pounds (181 kg) of food each day.

An elephant uses its trunk for eating. It grabs leaves and grass with its trunk. Then, it brings the leaves to its mouth. This is how the woolly mammoth ate.

An African elephant eating grass.

An elephant also uses its trunk for drinking. First, it sucks water into its trunk. Then, it brings the water to its mouth. This is how the woolly mammoth drank water, too.

Special Teeth

What did the woolly mammoth use its tusks for? Scientists believe they used their tusks to move snow. This would uncover grass for it to eat.

Today's elephants fight, dig, and rip bark with their tusks. Maybe woolly mammoths did these things, too.

The woolly mammoth had large teeth inside its mouth. There were two upper teeth and two lower teeth. Each tooth was about the size of a shoebox.

A woolly mammoth tooth fossil.

The woolly mammoth ground food between its teeth. This wore down their teeth over time. New teeth growing underneath pushed out the old, worn teeth. Like elephants today, woolly mammoths could grow six sets of teeth.

Woolly Mammoth's World

Woolly mammoths lived through many Ice Ages. During an Ice Age, the world became cooler. Giant sheets of ice covered many lands. The woolly mammoth's hairy coat and fat kept it warm.

The Pleistocene World

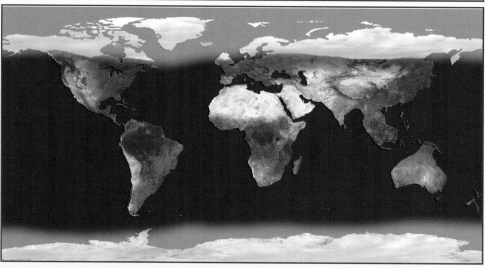

Ice covered parts of the world during the Pleistocene.

Woolly mammoths lived in Europe, North America, and northern Asia. They lived on grass steppes. This land had mixed grasses and few trees.

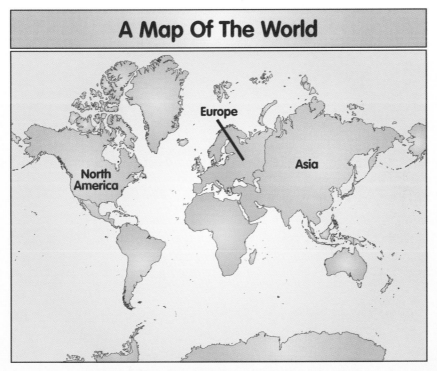

A Map Of The World

Europe

North America

Asia

Woolly mammoth fossils have been found in North America, Asia, and Europe.

Prehistoric people lived among woolly mammoths. They may have hunted woolly mammoths by trapping them in pits. Scimitar cats probably hunted the woolly mammoth's young.

Woolly mammoths died out about 9,000 years ago. No one is sure why this happened. Maybe an illness killed them. A climate change may have killed the plants they ate. Maybe prehistoric people hunted them all. Scientists hope to find the answer one day.

Discovering Jarkov

In 1997, Simion Jarkov was a nine-year-old boy. He lived in northern Siberia with his family. They were reindeer herders. One day, Simion found two giant tusks in the ice. They belonged to a woolly mammoth frozen in the ground.

Reindeer live in Siberia.

The frozen woolly mammoth was named Jarkov after the boy who found it. Scientists studying Jarkov hope to learn a lot from this exciting fossil. Jarkov may help them understand why woolly mammoths died out.

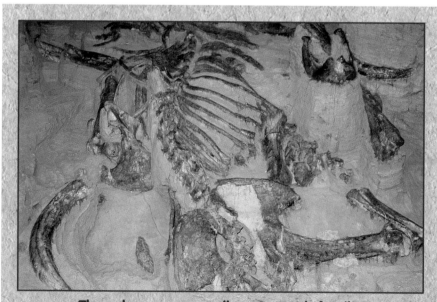

These bones are woolly mammoth fossils.

Important Words

climate the weather of a place over time.

fossil remains of very old animals and plants commonly found in the ground. A fossil can be a bone, a footprint, or any trace of life.

Ice Age a period in Earth's history when ice covered parts of the world. The last Ice Age ended about 11,500 years ago.

mammal most living things that belong to this special group have hair, give birth to live babies, and make milk to feed their babies.

prehistoric describes anything that was around more than 5,500 years ago.

tusks large teeth that stick out of an animal's mouth.

Web Sites

To learn more about woolly mammoths, visit ABDO Publishing Company on the World Wide Web. Web sites about woolly mammoths are featured on our Book Links page. These links are routinely monitored and updated to provide the most current information available.

www.abdopub.com

23

Index